ALASKA'S IDITAROD

BY EMILY SCHLESINGER

WHITE LIGHTNING BOOKS®

NONFICTION

Alaska's Iditarod

Children of the Holocaust

Cryptocurrency

Deadly Bites

Digital Worlds

Droids and Robots

Esports

Flight Squads

Navajo Code Talkers

Olympic Games

Stephen Hawking

Superbugs

The White House

Working Dogs

World Cup Soccer

SADDLEBACK
EDUCATIONAL PUBLISHING
www.sdlback.com

Photo credits: page 2: ventdusud / Shutterstock.com; pages 12/13: General Photographic Agency / Hulton Archive via Gettyimages.com; page 17: Max3105 / Shutterstock.com; pages 18/19: Troutnut / Shutterstock.com; page 27: Ezra Shaw / Getty Images Sport via Getty Images; page 40: Roger Asbury / Shutterstock.com; page 41: Roger Asbury / Shutterstock.com; pages 44-45: Frederic J. Brown / AFP via Getty Images; page 49: Ezra Shaw / Getty Images Sport via Getty Images

ISBN: 978-1-68021-883-1
eBook: 978-1-64598-207-4

Printed in Malaysia

25 24 23 22 21   1 2 3 4 5

Table of Contents

1 Nome Calling

It was January 1925. A **telegram** arrived at the governor's office in Juneau, Alaska. He picked it up. The words jumped off the page.

POSTAL TELEGRAPH COMMERCIAL CABLES

TELEGRAM

transmits and delivers this message subject to the terms and conditions printed o...blank.

Telegraph-Cable

COUNTER NUMBER.	TIME FILED.	CHECK.
12	5:00 M	

NOME CALLING . . .
NOME CALLING. . .
WE HAVE AN OUTBREAK OF DIPHTHERIA. . .
NO SERUM. . .
URGENTLY NEED HELP. . .

Nome calling . . .

Nome calling . . .

*We have an outbreak of **diphtheria** . . .*

*No **serum** . . .*

Urgently need help . . .

The governor slammed down the note. Nome was in trouble. Many in the city could die without medicine. There was not a minute to lose.

Disaster in Nome

Winter was harsh that year. Nome was completely cut off by ice and snow. The city lies in a remote corner of Alaska. Cars could not reach it. Trains and boats couldn't either.

Sick people there went to a doctor. They began to die one by one. The cause was diphtheria. It spread fast. There was a serum that could cure it. But the nearest supply was in Anchorage. This was 1,000 miles away.

DIPHTHERIA

Diphtheria is a respiratory disease caused by a bacteria that releases a poison into the body. It is especially deadly for children. The serum contained an antitoxin that could fight this poison.

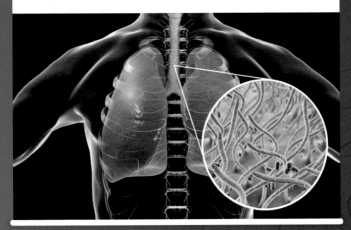

A team gathered in Juneau. They **brainstormed** what to do. How could they get the medicine across 1,000 miles of ice, snow, and mountains?

One possibility was to fly it. However, planes then were not made to fly in winter. Their cockpits were open. The air was too cold. A pilot would not survive.

There was another possibility. Sled dog teams traveled to Nome each month. They delivered mail. The route was called the Iditarod Trail. Sled drivers were called **mushers**. A musher might be able to deliver the medicine.

FAST FACT: Nome is a remote community on the western coast of Alaska. There are no roads that connect the town with the rest of the state. The only ways in and out of Nome are by airplane, dogsled, or boat.

This plan could work. But there was one problem. It took almost a month to make the trip using one sled team. The people of Nome did not have that long.

Then someone had a different idea. What if they created a relay race? Dog teams could wait in villages along the way. One team would hand off the serum to the next. That way each team would only have to run a short distance. The dogs would always be fresh. Little time would be lost to sleep.

This seemed like the best plan. Twenty dog teams were put into action. The first musher left on January 27, 1925.

The Serum Run

William "Wild Bill" Shannon hitched up his dog team. He was the first musher in the relay. The serum was packed on his sled.

A storm was growing. The temperature fell to 60 degrees below zero. People warned Shannon to wait. He refused. "People are dying," he said. "Let's get started."

Shannon's team ran 52 miles through the storm. Nine dogs were with him when he set out. Only six survived. They brought the medicine to Tolovana. Another musher carried it to Manley Hot Springs. The next team brought it to Fish Lake. On and on, the relay continued. Hundreds of miles were covered.

On January 30, Charlie Evans took over. The weather got worse. Two of his dogs froze while they ran. Evans stepped out of the sled. He put on one of their **harnesses**. Then he helped pull the sled himself.

A Dangerous Crossing

It was January 31, 1925. A musher named Leonhard Seppala took over. He was near Norton Sound. This is an inlet of the Bering Sea.

The storm was growing even more violent. Seppala saw an opportunity. There was a shortcut. His team could cross over Norton Sound. Its surface was frozen. This would save them time. It was risky, though. What if the ice broke? Then the medicine would be lost. Many people would die without it.

Seppala took the chance. He trusted his dogs. They led him across the ice with great skill. The team made it to the other side just in time. Three hours later, the ice broke.

FAST FACT: Mushers cross the Norton Sound at Norton Bay. This stretch of the trail is approximately 50 miles long and can take five to nine hours to cross depending on weather conditions.

The Last Stretch

Gunnar Kaasen was last in the relay. His lead dog was named Balto. A blizzard raged around them. Kaasen could barely see. There was a river ahead. But it was hidden from view. The team was about to plunge in. Balto sensed the danger. He brought the whole team to a sudden stop. This quick action saved their lives.

The danger was still not over. Soon the winds reached hurricane force. They lifted the whole team into the air. Everyone crashed back to the ground. It was a tangled mess. Kaasen panicked. Where was the serum?

Kaasen searched through the snow. Finally, he found it. He got his team back on the trail. By the end of the night, they reached Nome. They delivered the serum. The people of Nome were saved. Balto and Kaasen became heroes. It had taken just six days to complete the whole journey.

BALTO THE HERO

Balto became famous. He toured around the U.S. Big crowds came out to meet him. Several movies were made about his journey. In 1925, a statue of Balto was put up in Central Park in New York City. Today, Balto's body is on display at the Cleveland Museum of Natural History.

The Great Race

It was the 1960s. Forty years had passed. Some people still remembered Balto. But much of Alaska's dogsledding history had been forgotten. Now snowmobiles sped across the land.

One woman did not want people to forget. Her name was Dorothy Page. She had an idea. Alaska was about to celebrate its 100th year as part of the U.S. They could hold a huge sled dog race. This would follow the Iditarod Trail. It would honor the Serum Run of 1925.

Another Alaskan shared Page's dream. His name was Joe Redington. Together they got support for the project. Volunteers cleared the trail. The U.S. Army helped too. In 1973, the first Iditarod race was held.

Some thought the race would be too extreme. It went over some of the most remote terrain in the world. Temperatures were among the coldest anywhere. But the mushers and dogs proved they could do it. Twenty-two teams finished the first race. It has been held every year since.

The Route

Racers follow the path of the original Serum Run. It starts in Anchorage and ends in Nome. Altogether, the trail covers about 1,000 miles.

The beginning of the race is called the Ceremonial Start. It is like a parade. Teams run through the streets of Anchorage. Fans cheer them on. This part is not timed.

Then teams make their way to Willow Lake. This is the restart point. Timing begins here.

Part of the route heads over arctic tundra. It crosses mountain ranges and valleys. The Yukon River forms some of the trail. Teams race along its frozen surface. This is like a highway of ice.

FAST FACT: One thousand miles is about the distance from the Great Lakes to the Gulf of Mexico.

The Iditarod Route

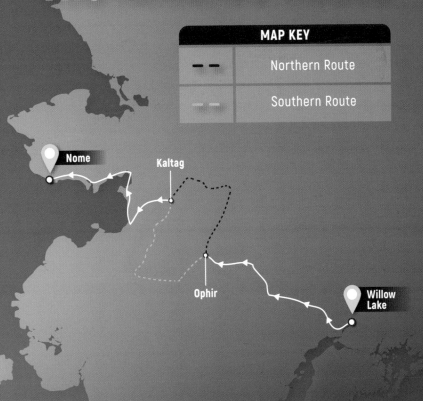

Nome

Kaltag

Ophir

Willow Lake

Later, the trail splits at Ophir. Some years, racers take a northern route. Other years, they go south. This spreads the impact of the race to other villages. Both routes meet in Kaltag. From there, teams follow the coast to Nome.

Who Can Race?

Anyone age 18 and up can enter the Iditarod. New mushers must run qualifying races and turn in a report card. Mushers can be male or female. Young and old can compete. One musher finished a race at age 84. Teams come from around the world.

The top 20 winners earn prize money. Each may get tens of thousands of dollars.

FAST FACT: About 30 percent of Iditarod participants are women. They are just as likely to finish in the top ten as the men.

THE JUNIOR IDITAROD

Beginning in 1976, a shorter version of the Iditarod was created for young people. This is called the Junior Iditarod. Teens ages 14 to 17 can enter. The distance is 150 miles. It takes place each year in late February.

Survival on the Trail

Mushers race alone. Conditions are brutal. It takes hard work and planning just to stay alive.

FAST FACT: In extremely cold conditions, it can take only minutes for frostbite to occur.

Most teams take between one and two weeks
to finish. That is a long time in the extreme cold.
Frostbite can result. **Hypothermia** is another risk.
High-tech clothing helps. Some wear animal fur.
Mushers build fires along the way to keep warm.
They sleep inside a bivy. This is a waterproof bag. It
zips like a tent.

Feeding the Team

A sled team may have 12 to 16 dogs. Each dog eats
up to 12,000 calories per day. This adds up to about
2,000 pounds of food per team.

It is too much to carry on a sled. Instead, mushers
pack food in bags before the race. Planes fly it to
checkpoints. These are stops along the way. There
are 25 in all. The food is waiting when they arrive.

The dogs eat a special **kibble**. This gives them energy. They also need many kinds of meat.

Mushers eat frozen meals. They heat them on camp stoves. Some like pizza. Others eat casseroles or cheesecake. High carbs and fat keep them going over long distances.

Keeping Safe

Dogs' feet can easily get hurt. That is why all the dogs wear tiny shoes. These are called booties. New ones are put on at each checkpoint. A team can use over 1,000 booties during a race.

EMERGENCY CARE

Mushers are supposed to handle all emergencies themselves. They bring tools to make repairs to sleds and harnesses. Injuries can happen too. Mushers act as veterinarians for their team. If a musher must call for help, there is a penalty.

CHAPTER 5

Born to Run

Blair Braverman is a musher. Her first Iditarod was in 2019. During the race, she tweeted about the experience. Fans loved it. Thousands began to follow her. She became a social media sensation.

400

646   1,2k   16,4k

Braverman tweets about her dogs' personalities. Boo "holds a lot of feelings in his small body," she writes. Colbert "is a big hunk of burning enthusiasm." Flame "is my souldog."

All of her dogs have different ways of communicating. Braverman pays close attention. One dog might look over her shoulder if there is a wild animal. Another might pick at his food when he is sick. Every burp is important, according to Braverman. She tries not to miss a signal. Learning her dogs' strengths and weaknesses is important too. This helps her put together the best team.

FAST FACT: Dogs need months of training to get ready for the Iditarod. Braverman's dogs ran 2,000 miles to get ready for the race.

94

157

198

SLED TEAM POSITIONS

Each dog has a position on the team. Lead dogs go in front. Their job is to find the way. This takes intelligence. Behind them are swing dogs. They steer. Next are the team dogs. These provide the team's muscle. Wheel dogs are the biggest. They take up the rear and get the sled moving.

A Breed Apart

Most racing dogs are mixed breeds. They are descended from Siberian huskies. This breed came from northeast Asia. The Chukchi people used them as sled dogs.

A fur trader brought the dogs to Alaska. There they mixed with Alaskan malamutes. These are also sled dogs. The result is known as the Alaskan husky. This is what most Iditarod dogs are today.

The dogs have many ways to stay warm. Thick coats hold in heat. Their feet have special blood vessels. These keep them from freezing. The dogs also have bushy tails. They put them over their noses at night. This traps warm air to breathe.

Alaskan huskies have another amazing quality. Their bodies can repair while they run. This means they need little rest. They can finish races fast.

BRED TO SLED

The Chukchi bred sled dogs for thousands of years. They selected them for certain traits. Dogs who had these traits were most likely to be kept for mating. They passed the traits on to their offspring. As a result, certain traits became stronger in each generation. One was friendliness. This made the dogs want to play and work with people. Intelligence was also important. The dogs had to be brave too. All of these traits make them ideal sled dogs.

Whatever It Takes

Sled dogs are tough. So are the humans driving them. Mushers need many qualities to survive. One of the most important is mental **stamina**.

Mushers learn to work through pain. They push through tiredness. Fears must be overcome. These leaders cannot buckle under pressure. Their teams' lives depend on it.

Many mushers only sleep two to three hours per night. Some keep an alarm clock inside their hats. After a short nap, they wake up and get back on the trail.

Staying alert is important. Dangers are everywhere. It is not just bad weather. There are wild animals too. Wolves, moose, and bison roam the land.

FAST FACT: Mushers are required to stop for one 24-hour rest period along the way. There are two other shorter rest periods. That way teams have a chance to recover without getting behind.

Runaway Dogs

Musher Linwood Fiedler recalls a scary moment. His sled hit a stump. Then all 13 dogs became detached. The dogs kept running. Fiedler was left alone in the dark. Dragging his sled, the musher looked for his team. But soon the weight was too much. He had to stop.

Moments later, another musher came by. He helped Fiedler search. Finally, they found the dogs. They had run five miles down the trail.

FAST FACT: Susan Butcher won the Iditarod four times.

On Thin Ice

Susan Butcher was racing with her team. Sea ice lay ahead. Her dogs dashed lightly over the surface. But Butcher's sled was too heavy. The ice cracked beneath it. Butcher and her sled plunged into arctic water. They were 30 feet from shore.

The musher had to think fast. "Haw!" she yelled. This was a signal to get moving. Her lead dogs ran as hard as they could. They pulled Butcher and the sled out of the water. She traveled the next ten miles soaking wet. But she was glad to be alive.

CHAPTER 7

A Will to Win

Mushers share one thing in common. It is a determination to test themselves against nature.

Several racers have stood out. Their will to win was unshakeable. It kept them going when others gave up.

Libby Riddles

It was 1985. Libby Riddles was racing in the Iditarod. A bad storm drew near. Teams began to pull off the trail. They waited out the storm.

Riddles knew she should do the same. But a question kept popping into her head. What if she were brave enough to take on the storm? Then she might win.

Temperatures were dangerous. They fell to 50 degrees below zero. Winds were near hurricane force. This was not just any blizzard. It was one of the worst in Iditarod history. Riddles decided to go right into the middle of it. She did what no one else dared.

Riddles got lost several times and almost gave up. It took hours to get through the storm. Finally she crossed the finish line. No one else was in sight. She became the first woman to win the Iditarod.

FAST FACT: Libby Riddles finished her Iditarod victory in 18 days, 20 minutes, and 17 seconds. In 2007, she was inducted into the Alaska Sports Hall of Fame.

Lance Mackey

One musher has been called "the toughest athlete on the planet." His name is Lance Mackey.

Mackey's first Iditarod was in 2001. He felt a terrible pain in his throat. It lasted the whole race. At the finish line, he collapsed. Doctors examined him. They found a softball-sized tumor. The musher began radiation treatment. Twelve teeth were pulled. His saliva glands were taken out too.

Doctors told Mackey he could not race again. His neck was held together with staples. He could bleed to death. The radiation damaged his skin. This made frostbite likely. Mackey's response was simple. "Don't tell me I can't," he said.

Mackey entered the next Iditarod. He could not chew or swallow. Instead, he used a feeding tube. It attached to his belly button.

Soon, he got frostbite. His ears, toes, and fingers were damaged. Later, Mackey lost the use of an arm. It was hard to hold the sled. He fell off often. The dogs would stop and wait for him.

During one race, his finger started hurting badly. Mackey stopped along the way. He found a surgeon. Then he had the finger amputated. After surgery, he got right back on the trail.

The musher kept racing year after year. Finally, his dream came true. In 2007, he won the Iditarod. He also won in 2008, 2009, and 2010.

Mackey became a four-time champion. His body held him back at every turn. But it was no match for his will.

FAST FACT: Lance Mackey has competed in 15 Iditarod races and won over $370,000 in prize money.

Tough Questions

People admire the strength of the mushers. In recent years, though, there has been **controversy**. Some ask if it is right to push the dogs so hard.

FAST FACT: PETA stands for People for the Ethical Treatment of Animals.

DOGS DRIVEN TO DEATH FOR IDITAROD
PeTA

CHRYSLER: STOP DRIVING DOGS TO THEIR DEATHS
END YOUR IDITAROD SPONSORSHIP
PeTA

Protesters have begun attending the Iditarod. They argue that the race is cruel. Many hold up signs. These show statistics. Over 150 dogs have died while racing. Some dogs also experience health problems each year.

Racing has dangers. Dogs can get tired or hurt. They can develop hypothermia. Some do not drink enough water. Fights might break out. A dog can get tangled in a harness.

One animal rights group is PETA. It is the largest in the world. PETA has taken a stand. The group wants the race to stop.

Mushers defend the sport. They say good care can keep dogs safe. Many point to recent numbers. The death rate of dogs has gone down. This shows the sport has gotten safer, they argue. A few racing dogs still die from injuries. Now, though, the rate is lower than it is for pets.

The Iditarod committee listens to both sides. They take the dangers seriously. New rules have been put into place. These improve safety for dogs.

SAFETY RULES

Many rules have been added to keep dogs safe. Now all dogs must have health checks before the race. Veterinarians work at checkpoints. Dogs receive care if they need it. Mushers must also complete a "Dog Team Diary" in which they write down health information about each dog. Mushers are trained in dog safety too. If proper care is not given, they can be punished.

Doping Scandal

Dogs get tested each year. Tests look for **doping** drugs. In 2017, four dogs failed for the first time ever. They had been given tramadol. This is an opioid. It kills pain.

This alarmed many people. Pushing through pain is dangerous. Serious injuries can result.

The dogs were on Dallas Seavey's team. He is a four-time Iditarod winner. His father, Mitch Seavey, is also a champion.

SPONSOR CHALLENGE

The Iditarod depends heavily on sponsors. Big-name companies donate money. This helps pay the costs of the race. It also allows for prize money. However, recent controversies have caused some sponsors to pull out. The Iditarod Committee has had to search for new sponsors to replace them.

Seavey denied giving his dogs the drug. He suggested someone else might have done it instead. Perhaps they wanted him out of the race.

The committee investigated. They could not find proof that Seavey did it. He was not punished. New rules were made. Now mushers are held responsible for positive drug test results.

A Changing Environment

The Iditarod faces another serious challenge. It is climate change. Temperatures have been rising in Alaska. This has affected the race.

Racers used to begin near Anchorage. But recently there has been too little snow. The starting point had to move 30 miles away to Willow Lake. Some years, even that did not work. Then teams had to start in Fairbanks. This is 300 miles north.

Trail Conditions

There have been other problems. Water crossings are no longer always frozen. Melted areas can be dangerous. Volunteers go out before each race. They put down logs. This makes bridges. Teams can then cross safely.

FAST FACT: In 2016, there was not enough snow in Anchorage to host the Ceremonial Start of the race. To fix this problem, 7,000 gallons of snow were imported for the event.

The Iditarod has a tradition. Teams cross Norton Sound. In 2019, this was not possible. There was not enough ice. Sea ice was at its lowest level in 150 years. Mushers had to go around.

Other parts of the trail have been completely dry. These areas might stretch as far as 20 miles. Only gravel and dirt cover them. Sleds can still run. But the ride is rough.

Warmer temperatures can harm dogs. They can overheat. Some mushers choose to run them at night. It is cooler then.

Climate Science

Scientists explain these changes. Temperatures have warmed since the race began. They have gone up about three degrees. This may not sound like a lot. But it can turn snow into slush. By 2050, the race may be six degrees warmer.

Moving the race north may be the answer. Many do not like that idea. The Iditarod is a historic race. It honors the Serum Run. Some worry its meaning would be lost if it moved.

FAST FACT: According to the National Oceanic and Atmospheric Administration, 2018 was Alaska's second-warmest year on record.

CHAPTER 1

The Iditarod Meets the Future

Many important questions have been raised about the Iditarod. This is partly because of the internet. It has spread interest far beyond Alaska. Today, people around the world follow the race.

FAST FACT: For most of the Iditarod's history, race updates and information were relayed by amateur HAM radio operators who would station themselves between race checkpoints.

The fan base is growing. Social media helps. Many mushers blog. Others tweet. Fans can follow them year-round. They get pumped up long before the race begins.

Staying Connected

Iditarod Insider reaches 164 countries. This is an online service. There, fans can track the race in real time. Reporters work at checkpoints. They interview mushers. People can also chat online with a digital sled dog mascot. Its name is Gia.

This connection was not always possible. For many years, radio was the only way to communicate. Now, satellite communication sends data fast. It works where cell phones do not.

Each musher carries a satellite phone. They can use it in emergencies. Sleds have **GPS** too. This makes sure no one goes missing.

A Winning Partnership

One thing has not changed. It is how much mushers love to race. Many see it as the highlight of their lives. Some enter year after year.

They say their dogs love it too. Racing is in the dogs' blood. Each husky comes from a long line of sled dogs. When they run, they are doing what they do best.

For thousands of years, humans and dogs have shared a bond. Dogsledding has helped people survive in harsh climates. The race celebrates this bond. It sends a message. Together, people and their dogs can go far. That is the spirit of the Iditarod.

MICROCHIPS AND SAFETY

Dr. Stuart Nelson serves as lead veterinarian for the Iditarod. He imagines a future where a microchip inside each dog sends health information to a dashboard on the musher's sled. That way the musher can keep track of each dog's health in real time.

Glossary

amputate: to cut off a part of the body for medical reasons

blizzard: a heavy snowstorm with strong winds

brainstorm: to come up with new ideas and creative solutions through group discussion

climate change: long-term changes in temperature and precipitation

controversy: an issue that the public disagrees strongly about

diphtheria: a bacterial disease that attacks the respiratory system

doping: using drugs to enhance performance in a sport

frostbite: a condition in which extreme cold damages skin tissue, sometimes permanently

GPS: stands for global positioning system; uses satellites to locate objects on Earth

harness: a set of straps attaching an animal to a sled or cart

hypothermia: a condition in which body temperature drops below a safe level

inlet: a part of a body of water that sticks out into the land

kibble: dog food made of ground-up ingredients shaped into pellets

musher: a person who drives a dogsled

protester: someone who goes to a public place to show disagreement by holding up signs or chanting

serum: a liquid taken from the blood of someone with immunity to a disease and injected in someone else to give them immunity

stamina: the ability to keep going

statistic: a fact that contains numerical data

telegram: a message sent over long distances using wires and electrical signals; an old-fashioned communication method

tundra: a large area of flat, frozen land with no trees found in northern parts of the world

TAKE A LOOK INSIDE

WORKING DOGS

CHAPTER 2

The Origin of Dogs

It was thousands of years ago. Early humans lived together. They made camp. A trash pile started. Gray wolves nosed around it. The animals wanted an easy meal. Some growled at people and bared their teeth. Most wolves were a threat. Men chased them away.

One small wolf did not growl. Many liked her. They fed her scraps. She stayed and had pups. The pups lived with the people too. These wolves became tame.

Is this where dogs came from? Scientists are not sure. More research is needed.

Helping Humans

The change to **domesticated** dog took time. Ears got floppy. Coats had more spots. **Personalities** changed. Dogs learned to obey humans. They lived together. People became their new packs.

FAST FACT: Scientists are not sure where dogs got their start. It could have been Europe or the Middle East. Others think it was East Asia.

CHAPTER 5

Search and Rescue Dogs

Thick snow covers a mountain. Then it begins to slide. This is an **avalanche**. People ski out of the way. Not all make it. One woman is buried in the snow. Her air will run out in minutes. She must get out.

This victim is lucky. Duke is on the job. He finds her scent. The dog digs until he reaches her. Rescuers pull her out.

Duke does search and rescue (SAR). These dogs work hard. One can do the work of 20 people. Many search in snow. Others search in forests. Some work in cities. Their goal is the same. They want to find a missing person.

FAST FACT: Dogs can smell a human under 15 feet of snow.

24   25

CHAPTER 10

Dogs with Unique Jobs

Most have heard of police dogs. Herders are common too. Service dogs are seen all over. But some dogs have unique jobs. They help in special ways.

Piper works at an airport. He does not sniff luggage. This dog works outside. The border collie scans the runway. His ears perk up. Geese land nearby. The dog takes off. He frightens the geese away. Now the runway is safe.

Chasing birds is Piper's job. He chases rodents too. This is because they attract birds. At airports, birds cause problems. They can **collide** with planes. That can damage planes. They might even crash. Dogs keep the runway clear. Not many dogs do this job. But their work is important.

FAST FACT: Dogs have been trained to sniff for diseases that kill bees.

52   53

WHITE LIGHTNING BOOKS® NONFICTION

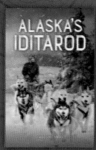

MORE TITLES COMING SOON

SDLBACK.COM/WHITE-LIGHTNING-BOOKS